Meet the Incredible Romans

Pictures by
Simon Abbott

Words by
John Malam

A City Called Rome

The Romans built a huge empire and ruled it for hundreds of years from a city called Rome, in Italy. Let's find out more about the ancient city.

Legend has it that Rome was built by twins - **Romulus** and **Remus**. The brothers fought over the name of the city, and Romulus killed Remus. Romulus called the city Rome, after himself.

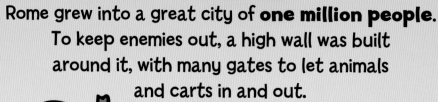

Watch it, bro!

Rome grew into a great city of **one million people**. To keep enemies out, a high wall was built around it, with many gates to let animals and carts in and out.

FUN FACTS

The Roman Empire was criss-crossed by **roads** - about 50,000 miles in total - and they were nearly always straight lines!

Rome had lots of **grand buildings**, markets and squares. There were big houses for **rich** people to live in, and thousands of small apartments where **poorer** people lived.

The area the Romans conquered was called the **Roman Empire**. It covered a large part of Europe, and parts of Africa and Asia. About **50 million** people lived in the empire.

Where next?

THE ROMAN EMPIRE

ROME

ITALY

A big **drain** underneath Rome, wider than a boat, flushed wee and poo into the River Tiber!

In Rome there was a golden **milestone** carved with the names of the empire's cities, with their distances from Rome.

WOW!

Roman Rulers

The empire was ruled by a powerful man called the emperor. He was in charge of everything. Some emperors were good and were liked by the people, but others treated people badly.

AUGUSTUS

Emperor Augustus was the first emperor. He made Rome into a beautiful city full of grand buildings. People liked him because he gave them **free bread** every day!

Emperor Caligula put up the price of food, which made him very unpopular. He spent money on silly things, such as keeping his favourite **horse** in a white marble stable.

CALIGULA

FUN FACTS

Emperor Nero thought he could sing. He wouldn't let people leave a theatre until they had listened to his terrible singing!

Emperor Claudius didn't want to be an emperor. He hid behind a curtain, but soldiers found him and made him the new emperor!

When there was a lot of fighting in the Roman Empire, **Emperor Hadrian** brought peace. In Britain he ordered a wall to be built. **Hadrian's Wall** showed where the Roman Empire stopped.

HADRIAN

COMMODUS

Emperor Commodus thought he was a living god. He renamed Rome **Commodiana**, after himself! No one liked the new name, and they didn't like the emperor much either!

Emperor Valerian was taken prisoner by a Persian king, who used him as a step to mount his horse!

Keep steady!

Emperor Romulus Augustulus was the last emperor. He was just 16!

WOW!

Ferocious Fighting!

Gladiator games were very popular. They were held in big arenas in front of huge crowds. Everyone came to watch gladiators fight!

There were many types of gladiator...

A '**net man**' used a net, a three-pronged spear called a trident and a dagger. He tried to catch his opponent with his net.

Hit him!

Hit him harder!

A '**chaser**' ran around a lot, chasing his opponent. He wore a helmet, and carried a rectangular shield and sword.

The Colosseum was the largest arena in the Roman Empire and could hold up to **80,000** people!

At the end of a fight, the crowd decided if a gladiator should **live** or **die**. They made signs with their thumbs to show what they thought should happen to the loser!

The **'blind-fighter'** couldn't see a thing! His helmet covered his face and there were no eye holes. He fought another 'blind-fighter' - they stumbled around until they bumped into each other!

Ready, Steady, Go!

Some cities in the Roman Empire had a track to race chariots. On a race day, thousands of people went to cheer and watch the action-packed races.

Stop horsing around!

In a race, there were **four** teams – the **Reds**, the **Whites**, the **Blues** and the **Greens**. The Romans supported chariot teams and wore their team's colours like people support sports teams today.

Up to three chariots from each team took part in a race, each pulled by two, three or four horses. When the **race starter** dropped a white cloth, off they went!

C'mon, Speedy!

FUN FACTS

Chariots raced **seven times** around the big racetrack in Rome. A race lasted for about nine minutes.

A charioteer called **Pompeius Musclosus** who raced for the Blue team won an incredible 3,559 races!

The racetrack was long and narrow, with sharp bends at each end.
Crashes happened at the bends – which made the race exciting to watch!

It was hard work holding onto the reins.
The winner was given a **palm leaf** as a prize.

A chariot's top speed was around **46 miles per hour** – about as fast as a lion runs!

In between chariot races, **acrobats** entertained the crowd by jumping between the moving horses!

Quick March!

The Romans had a big, strong army. Their soldiers marched all over the Roman Empire, fought in lots of battles and conquered many lands.

When a new soldier joined the Roman army he was given a **helmet** to protect his head and **armour** to cover his shoulders, chest and back. He wore a short '**skirt**' made from strips of leather, and leather **boots**.

Ready for kit inspection!

A soldier fought with a short **sword**, a **dagger** and a **javelin**. He carried a long, rectangular **shield**.

The **centurion** was the tough commander of a group of soldiers.

I'm the boss!

Hornblowers were noisy musicians who blew on big, curly horns.

Legionaries were the ordinary soldiers of the Roman army.

The **standard bearer** carried a pole which displayed the badges of his soldiers.

FUN FACTS

Did You Know?
Soldiers often held their shields above their heads, making a **tortoise** shape to protect them from spears and arrows.

A Roman **catapult** hurled big stones that punched holes through enemy walls.

WOW!

A Roman **javelin** was built to bend or snap on impact, so the enemy couldn't throw it back!

Soldiers weren't just fighters - they were **builders**! They built roads and bridges, and forts to live in.

Meet the Neighbours

Rome was an overcrowded, busy city, where rich people and poor people lived close together. They had very different homes and led very different lives.

The richest people lived in **private houses** with rooms built around an open courtyard. The floors were decorated with tiny pieces of coloured stone called **mosaics**.

Rich Romans owned **slaves**, and they were put to work on farms, in mines, and in people's homes. Some slaves were trained to fight as gladiators.

The grandest houses had their own private toilets connected to the city's **drains**.

The poorest people lived in **apartment blocks**. An apartment was just one room for a whole family to live in, and it was dark, smelly and noisy. There were **shops** on the ground floor.

There were no **toilets** in the rooms. People had to share potties on the landings. When they were full, they were emptied onto the street below!

Oi! Do you mind?

Bread for sale!

Bath Time!

The Romans believed in keeping themselves clean. They went to the town baths a lot - not only to swim, but to wash and catch up with friends!

Women and old people went to the baths in the morning, and men went in the afternoon, after they had finished work.

In the **changing room** they took off all their clothes - they all swam naked!

Phew!

In the **hot room**, olive oil was poured onto their bodies, then was scraped off to get rid of all the dirt.

In the **steam room** they sweated a lot to get dirt and grime out of their skin.

FUN FACTS

Air was heated in a **furnace** to warm the water, and came out of the walls to make the hot rooms really hot.

People were given sandals with **wooden soles** to stop their feet burning on the hot floor!

In the **cold room** they jumped into a pool of cold water.

Not too hot... and not too cold!

Brrrrrr!

In the **cool room** they soaked themselves in a pool of lukewarm water.

In the **massage room** they had sweet-smelling oil rubbed into their skin.

Barbers cut men's hair - and plucked hairs out of their ears and noses! Ouch!

The biggest baths in Rome covered 27 acres - that's about 15 football pitches!

WOW!

Looking to the Gods

The Romans believed in 12 main gods, and lots of minor gods. They thought the gods controlled everything in the world.

The Romans built grand **temples** to their gods as a home for them on earth. Priests and priestesses worked at the temples, and people left **gifts** at the temples to please the gods.

Jupiter was the king of all the gods, and controlled the **weather**. He sent rain and sunshine, stamped his feet to make thunder and threw bolts of lightning when he was angry.

Juno was the queen of the gods and married to Jupiter. She protected **women**, **children** and marriage. The month of **June** is named after her.

FUN FACTS

Priests thought they could see into the future by inspecting the **guts** of dead animals. Yuck!

I promise it won't hurt!

Neptune was the god of the **sea**. He travelled the oceans on a dolphin or sea horse. He also made earthquakes happen, so Romans called him the 'shaker of the earth'.

Mars was the god of **war**, battles and weapons. He was also the god of farming. The month of **March** is named after him.

Apollo was the god of **healing** and medicine, and could look into the future. He was also the **sun god**, who gave light and warmth to the world.

Cupid was the god of love. Anyone hit by one of his arrows fell madly in love.

The Roman god **Janus** had two faces – one looking forwards to the future, the other looking backwards to the past.

WOW!

Meal Time!

In Rome, most people bought takeaway food at the city's bakeries and taverns. Food was served all day long, and people ate sausages, pies, stews, cakes and pastries.

The Romans had a small **breakfast** of bread, cheese, fruit and water.

Lunch was a light meal of yesterday's leftovers - such as meat or fish eaten with bread and wine.

The **main meal** was eaten at about 3 o'clock in the afternoon. If it was a banquet, it could last for **hours**!

A banquet started with **snails**, **shellfish**, oysters, boiled eggs, figs and wine.

Dinner is served!

Cheers!

Rich Romans held **banquets** in their homes. Guests did not sit on chairs at a table but laid on **couches**, propped up on their elbows.

More wine, please!

The main course was **roast pig, peacocks**, fish, cabbage and more wine.

Then they had **fresh fruit**, nuts and cakes - and even more wine!

At the end of the banquet, guests sang songs and played games.

Food! Glorious food!

Ancient Roman Facts

For hundreds of years, men and boys wore **togas**. But togas went out of fashion, replaced by **tunics** which were much easier to put on!

People thought an **owl** hooting was a sign of danger – but believed if they spat three times, the danger would go away!

The Romans didn't use **toilet paper**. Instead, they used small sponges on the end of sticks!

Julius Caesar was a powerful general with a bald head. He combed his hair from the back or wore a wreath of **laurel leaves** to hide his bald patch!

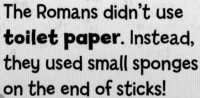

Who are you calling 'Baldy'?

BALDIUS HEADIUS

At the theatre, actors wore **masks** to show the audience whether they were playing happy or sad characters.